MARX

A BEGINNER'S GUIDE

GILL HANDS

Hodder & Stoughton

A MEMBER OF THE HODDER HEADLINE GROUP

Orders: please contact Bookpoint Ltd, 130 Milton Park, Abingdon, Oxon OX14 4SB. Telephone: (44) 01235 827720, Fax: (44) 01235 400454. Lines are open from 9.00–6.00, Monday to Saturday, with a 24-hour message answering service. Email address: orders@bookpoint.co.uk

British Library Cataloguing in Publication Data
A catalogue record for this title is available from The British Library

ISBN 0 340 78013 4

First published 2000
Impression number   10 9 8 7 6 5 4 3
Year   2005 2004 2003 2002

Cartoons by Richard Chapman
Typeset by Transet Limited, Coventry, England.
Printed in Great Britain for Hodder & Stoughton Educational, a division of Hodder Headline Plc, 338 Euston Road, London NW1 3BH by Cox & Wyman, Reading, Berks

Acknowledgments

I would like to thank my family and friends for their support and advice during the preparation of this book. I am especially grateful to my husband, Brian, for his computer expertise and to my daughter, Karen, for doing the washing up and initiating me into the mysterious world of the Internet!

CONTENTS

PREFACE

In a survey, commissioned by the BBC in 1999, Karl Marx was voted the greatest thinker of the last thousand years. He is certainly a well-known figure, but what did he actually believe? There are many books about Marx on the market that assume the reader already has an understanding of economics and philosophy, others are written by academics for academics, who already know what Marx wrote and wish to discuss the finer points of his ideas in detail. This book aims to give an understanding of the key areas of Marx's philosophy and show how his ideas have affected the world we live in today.

Marx – A Beginner's Guide is organized into 7 chapters, key facts and ideas are highlighted throughout, and each chapter ends with a summary. The first chapter introduces Marx the man, examining his life and its historical context. The second chapter discusses the influence of other philosophers in the development of his thought. Chapters 3, 4, 5 and 6 look in more detail at his philosophy and his economic and historical ideas. The final chapter looks at the ways in which his ideas influenced the history of the world, and their relevance and importance to the lives of people in the twenty-first century.

If you have ever wondered what the *Communist Manifesto* was, why it was written and what it said; if you want to know what Marx thought about religion, alienation or revolution; if you've always wondered what ideology and the dictatorship of the proletariat are; this book is for you.

Marx's Life and Times

Karl Marx is sometimes known as the father of **communism**. Although he did not invent the idea of communism, he was the first person to develop the idea and write about it in a practical and scientific way. He lived and wrote in the nineteenth century, but it was not until the twentieth century that his ideas became widespread and led to **revolution**. During his lifetime, his philosophy was mainly known only to **radical** thinkers and political activists. Today most people in the world have at least heard the name Marx, though they may only have a vague understanding of what he believed.

Marx wrote many articles and books throughout his life; the most well known are:

* *The Communist Manifesto*: written in 1848 with **Friedrich Engels**;

* *Das Kapital*: written between the 1850s and his death in 1883. The final volumes were completed by Engels.

EUROPE AT THE TIME OF MARX

Karl Marx was born on 5 May 1818 at Trier in the Rhineland, which was then a part of Prussia. His father, Heinrich Marx, was a lawyer. Although the family were of the Jewish faith, Heinrich Marx registered as a Protestant Christian when laws were passed preventing Jews from holding public positions. There was much anti-Jewish feeling in the Rhineland at that time, and many Jews felt oppressed by the government. This must have left some impression on Marx although he was never a devout religious believer.

The world that Marx lived in was very different from the Western Europe of today. In order to understand what Marx believed, and why he believed it, we need to look at the society in which he lived and the influence it had upon him.

Marx grew up in a time of rapid social change throughout Europe. The main forces for this change were:

* the Industrial Revolution, which had started in Britain. This led to the growth of the factory system throughout Europe;

* the French Revolution of 1789 and the Napoleonic Wars (1799–1815) which led to the downfall of the monarchy and the abolition of **feudalism** throughout much of Europe.

> **KEYWORD**
>
> Feudalism: a system of land ownership that gave the nobility rights over the land, which they granted to their followers in return for services.

Huge cities were growing up throughout the Western world, and the invention of the steam engine and the growth of factories all meant that people lived in a completely different way to their ancestors. In the past, people lived in close-knit communities and worked in traditional agriculture or as craftsmen. The rapid growth of factories meant that many independent craftsmen and small workshops disappeared.

Agricultural reforms and machinery increased the efficiency of farms and led to unemployment in rural areas. Landowners also took over the common lands and grazing rights which had belonged to the poor; this in turn increased rural poverty.

The new cities and factory towns were soon flooded with destitute farmers, craftsmen and their families. They were desperate to work under any conditions, living in slum housing and working long hours in factories or mines with unguarded and dangerous machinery. There were no safety regulations and even young children had to work. Soon the workers began to group together into unions to lobby for better working conditions. Although Prussia was mainly backward and agricultural, the Rhineland was the most industrialized area. Marx was able to study both the lives of peasant wine growers and the factory workers in his own area and see how unjust the system was.

The area where Karl Marx grew up had been under French domination for many years and the young middle classes were inspired by the example of the French Revolution of 1789. This had overthrown the ruling classes of the nobility and clergy to replace them with the middle classes or bourgeoisie. The Napoleonic Wars spread the ideas and institutions of post-revolutionary France through much of Europe including Prussia.

ACADEMIC LIFE

Marx followed in his father's footsteps and in 1835 registered as a law student at the University of Bonn, although he later became more interested in history and philosophy. His academic career was rather chequered. He did not spend much time on his studies and became involved in a duelling society, where he was wounded in the eye by an unknown member. His father insisted he should stop his wild rampaging and move to a place with a more academic atmosphere.

> **KEYWORD**
>
> Hegel: German philosopher (1770–1831). His writings on the progress of civilization and its conflicts influenced Marx and are explained in greater detail in Chapter 2.

In 1836 he entered the University of Berlin. He started to become more interested in the philosophy of law than in the study of law itself. He became increasingly interested in the teachings of **Hegel** and was a prominent member of the Young Hegelians, a group of radicals with views that the establishment saw as unorthodox.

Between 1838–1840 he wrote a thesis on Greek philosophers, which was accepted at the University of Jena in 1841.

LIFE AS A JOURNALIST

Marx hoped to take up a university teaching post after his studies, but because of his association with the Young Hegelians and other radical thinkers he was unsuccessful.

Marx married Jenny von Westphalen in 1843. She was the beautiful young daughter of Baron von Westphalen, a cultured and politically progressive Prussian aristocrat. The Baron had encouraged Marx in his childhood studies, advising him to read Greek poetry and Shakespeare.

In the same year Marx began work for the radical paper *Rheinische Zeitung*. He was a political journalist and arguably invented documentary reporting, writing several hard-hitting articles on the plight of the peasants in the Moselle region of France. One of the problems there was the prosecution of poor people. In the past it had been one of the common rights of peasants under the feudal system to be allowed to gather firewood. When the land passed into private ownership they had to pay for the wood and most could not afford to. Marx did not hesitate to criticize the government on this and other matters in his writing. The paper was eventually censored and Marx was forced to resign. The paper was later closed down.

During his time at the paper Marx realized that his knowledge of economic and social matters was not very wide and he began to study political economy seriously. He saw that society was unfair and wished for change, but he realized none of the current philosophies explained how the changes he wished for could come about. He felt that philosophy was not scientific enough and that philosophy in itself was not enough to change the world. Action would need to be taken!

In the autumn of 1843 he moved to Paris to escape the restrictions imposed by the government. He worked on a new journal, the German-French *Annals*. Although it only ran for one issue, because of distribution problems, it was important because it was the first time that Marx had directed his appeals at the workers rather than just at intellectuals.

It was during his time at the paper that Marx reacquainted himself with Friedrich Engels, who was to become his lifelong friend and co-writer. Engels had been working as a business agent in his father's branch office in England where he had seen the poverty and deprivation of the working class at first hand. In 1944–1945, he wrote *The Condition of the Working Classes in England* which condemned the society of the time. Engels sent an article on economics to the German-French *Annals* which impressed Marx and they soon became close friends.

During his time in Paris, Marx became even more radical. He came under the influence of Russian **anarchists**, including Mikhail Bakunin. Anarchists believe:

KEYWORD

Anarchists: believers in the theory that society does not need government.

* society does not need government;

* no government is legitimate unless consented to by all those it governs;

* freedom is absolute: no one should be obliged to obey authority without freely consenting to do so.

These ideals were to become more important to Marx as he struggled to work out his own philosophy.

THE COMMUNIST MANIFESTO

Together, Marx and Engels worked out their own theory of reform and in 1848 they published a small booklet, *The Communist Manifesto*. It was written for the Communist League, a society that they had both joined in 1848, and was the first full statement of their world view. It described the unfair state of society and how it could be changed by revolution into an ideal communist state.

The Communist Manifesto was a document which:

KEYWORDS

Capitalist: economic system where there is private property and relatively free markets where goods are sold for profit.

Proletariat: the property-less working class in a capitalist system.

Bourgeoisie: the middle classes who developed capitalism and took power from the aristocrats.

* described the **capitalist** system of the times and how it had come about;
* described the **proletariat** and how it was created;
* examined the conflict between the proletariat and the **bourgeoisie**;
* presented the objections others had to communism and criticized them;
* put forward the idea of revolution and explained how communism would work.

It contained the famous phrase (which is often misquoted): 'The proletarians have nothing to lose but their chains. They have a world to win. Working men of all countries unite!'

Because of his revolutionary ideas Marx was becoming more of a threat to the established order. He was asked to leave several European countries because of his views, and was expelled from France in 1845, from Belgium in 1848, and from Prussia in 1849.

LIFE IN LONDON

In 1849 Marx moved to London with his wife and children. His wife actually gave birth to seven children throughout their marriage, but only three survived. It is alleged that he also had an illegitimate son by his wife's maid, Helene. His main source of income came from writing articles for papers such as *The New York Tribune*. Unfortunately, he was unable to write in English at first and he relied on the help of Engels as translator. Engels was an excellent linguist – his friends said he knew how to stammer in twelve languages!

Engels also helped by lending money to the Marx family who lived in extreme poverty when they first lived in London. Often they lived on nothing but bread and potatoes and three children died because of poor diet and lack of medicines; money even had to be borrowed for their funerals. Marx was a frequent visitor to the pawn shop where he pawned

whatever he could, including his clothes. This way of life was especially difficult for Marx's wife, Jenny, who came from a wealthy background. She wrote to a friend, Joseph Weydemeyer, '… two bailiffs came and confiscated all my few possessions – linen, beds, clothes – everything – even my poor child's cradle and my daughters' best toys; they stood there weeping bitterly.'

Marx spent the last 25 years of his life working on *Das Kapital*, a scientific study of capitalism, politics and economics which ran into several volumes. He often worked in the British Museum Library and became a well-known figure there. The museum had collections of factory inspectors', and public health officers' reports that he used for research purposes.

He also became known to more working people and activists through public speaking at working men's clubs and to political groups. However, he was fiercely argumentative and often quarrelled with members of the groups he worked with. He often publicly attacked those he did not agree with. For example, he wrote a criticism of the nineteenth-century French philosopher Pierre Joseph Proudhon and got into a legal battle with Karl Vogt, a left-wing German politician. He was often seen in public life as being bad tempered, but in private he was a loving and gentle husband and father.

His final years were dogged by illness, especially bronchitis – he was a heavy smoker and often joked that the money he made from *Das Kapital* was not enough to pay for the tobacco he smoked while writing it. He also enjoyed drinking alcohol, sometimes to excess! Other illness were often made worse by overwork. He was spending more and more time addressing meetings as well as writing. Much of his time was taken up with the International Working Men's Association, or the International as it became known. This had been founded in London in 1864, at a public meeting to which Marx was invited. He was elected to the General Council, wrote its inaugural address and drew up its statutues.

His wife died in 1881 and his beloved eldest daughter died a year later. Marx never really recovered from these deaths and he died himself in March 1883. After his death Engels spent 11 years working on his papers and completing the final volumes of *Das Kapital*.

Marx's ideas spread around the world very slowly but became known to most of the world after the Russian Revolution of 1917. Many revolutions have been started in the name of Marx, but no country has ever had the truly communist society, where social classes cease to exist, that Marx had hoped for. He is often seen as some kind of superhuman revolutionary figure who could do no wrong, though Marx himself often said his favourite motto was, 'I am a man and nothing human is alien to me'.

******SUMMARY******

- Karl Marx was born in 1818 in Trier, Germany.

- He was the first person to write about communism in a practical and scientific way.

- His best known works are *The Communist Manifesto* and *Das Kapital*.

- He lived through a time of rapid industrialization and social change in Europe.

- He was exiled from Germany as a radical.

- He was influenced by many philosophers, including Hegel.

- He had a close friend and co-writer, Friedrich Engels.

- He lived in London with his wife and family in extreme poverty.

- He died in 1883.

2 Who influenced Marx?

Marx is seen by some as a great **philosopher** and by others as a great **economist**. He was in fact both of these things, although he claimed to have little time for most of the philosophers who went before him: 'The philosophers have only interpreted the world in different ways; the point is to change it' he said in one of his *Theses on Feuerbach*, the German philospher. This is sometimes seen as a statement that he was totally against the study of philosophy and

KEYWORDS

Philosopher: a person who uses reason and argument to seek truth and knowledge.

Economist: a person who studies the science of the production and distribution of wealth.

saw it as a waste of time. In fact, he believed that philosophy should be made clearer by scientific study and then used to bring about social change.

His interest in the serious study of philosophy began while he was at the University of Berlin, and he wrote his doctoral thesis on the contrasts between two ancient Greek philosophers, Democtritus and Epicurus. Marx saw parallels between the thoughts of these ancient philosophers and the interpretation of Hegel's philosophy. Hegel was an important figure in Germany at that time and his ideas were hotly debated by students, who even then liked to sit around discussing what a terrible state the world was in and how they would like to change it. When Marx's father accused him of debauchery in a dressing gown he probably had no idea that his son would be one of the few students who would go on to change the world in a significant way!

The main debate between the philosophers of the time covered two

main schools of thought.

* **Idealist philosophers**: who assume there is a divine force of some kind which is responsible for the development of ideas and beliefs among mankind.

* **Materialist philosophers**: who believe that all ideas and beliefs come out of life and its conditions and not from any divine being or supernatural force.

The debate between idealists and materialists had been recorded since the time of the ancient Greeks, but it had been renewed by the popularity of Hegel in Germany at the time Marx was a student. It is easier to understand the importance of the debate, and of the development of Hegel's philosophy by Marx, if we look at the development of philosophy up to the nineteenth century.

A BRIEF HISTORY OF PHILOSOPHY

As philosophy tries to explain the truth behind life itself it must have been around for as long as mankind has existed. The earliest people had no means of recording what they believed so we can only surmise that they were superstitious and tried to explain natural phenomena as products of some divine force. Natural elements such as fire and water were worshipped as gods and, from this, organized religion developed.

The first philosophers, as we understand the term today, were ancient Greeks who started by criticizing religious beliefs. They used the scientific knowledge that was available to them at the time to explain the world around them and this sometimes brought them into conflict with organized religion and led to persecution.

The conflict between organized religion and freethinkers went on for centuries. In Europe, the dominance of the Christian Church did not encourage the development of philosophical thought. Anyone who did not agree with orthodox Christian doctrines was likely to be branded as a heretic and tortured to death.

It was not until the fifteenth century that freer debate began, and it was not until the French and American revolutions in the eighteenth century that the Church began to lose its dominance over the thoughts of the masses.

The materialist philosophers of the eighteenth and nineteenth centuries debated the existence of God and whether this could be proved by scientific means. Scientific development at that time was in the fields of mathematics and mechanical laws. This influenced the world view of the philosophers who saw society as fixed and

KEYWORD

Dialectic: the philosophic theory of contradiction and change.

unchanging, believing it followed immutable scientific rules. It meant that people believed they had a fixed place in society which could not be altered. It was not until Hegel developed the idea of the **dialectic** that people began to understand that nothing was constant and that they themselves had a part to play in influencing the course of history.

WHICH PHILOSOPHERS INFLUENCED MARX?

Marx did not arrive at his own philosophy without studying, and being influenced by, those who went before him. In a letter to his friend Weydemeyer in 1852 wrote, 'no credit is due to me for discovering the existence of classes ... nor yet the struggle between them'. Philosophers in the distant past, such as Aristotle (384–322 BC), had seen the influence of class. Marx analysed the ideas of philosophers from the past and certain groups of thinkers became more important to him, including:

* Greek philosophers;
* French materialists;
* German materialists;
* English philosophers and social reformers;
* Russian anarchists.

Among these groups there were individuals whose ideas can be seen to have definitely influenced the philosophy of Marx:

Democritus (c. 460–370BC)
Ancient Greek materialist philosopher who believed that the world could be explained by scientific laws, although science at the time was not advanced enough for him to be able to prove his theory.

Epicurus (341–271BC)
Greek philosopher who believed that if the world operates on mechanical principles then death and the gods are not to be feared. He thought this freedom from fear would allow people to live in peaceful communes devoted to pleasure.

Aristotle (384–322BC)

Greek philosopher, scientist and teacher. He realized that conflict in society often came from economic conditions and inequality in the structure of society.

Renée Descartes (1596–1650)
French philosopher and mathematician. The father of modern philosophy. He believed that philosophy and knowledge could be unified and classified by mathematical means.

John Locke (1632–1704)
English philosopher and physician. He believed that religion did not hold the absolute truth and that knowledge '…is founded on and ultimately derives from sense'. His belief in social equality – 'we are all equal, of the same species and condition … with equal right to enjoy the fruits of nature' – and his belief that if the rulers of society offend against natural law they must be deposed, were to be a powerful influence on the American and French Revolutions.

Robert Owen (1771–1858)
Welsh social reformer who believed character was formed by social conditions. He built a model community with schools and good housing for the workers in his mill.

Charles Fourier (1772–1837)
French social theorist who believed society should be reorganized into self-sufficient units or communes with communal property and consumer co-operatives for the redistribution of wealth.

Georg Wilhelm Friedrich Hegel (1770–1831)
German philosopher who believed civilization progressed through intellectual development and saw the history of society as a series of conflicts or dialectics. A major influence on Marx.

Ludwig Andreas Feuerbach (1804–1872)

German philosopher and student of Hegel. His most famous work, *The Essence of Christianity*, proposed that religion is 'the dream of the human mind', in other words that man creates an illusory God based on human ideals and experiences.

Louis Auguste Blanqui (1805–1881)
French revolutionary and extremist who believed in violent revolution and was the first to speak of the power of the proletariat.

Pierre Joseph Proudhon (1809–1865)
French anarchist who is famous for the saying 'property is theft'. This cry was taken up by revolutionary communists and is often wrongly attributed to Marx.

Louis Blanc (1811–1882)
French socialist and leader of workers' groups. He believed social equality should come about by democratic and peaceful means. His best known saying is: 'From each according to his ability, to each according to his needs.' This was another cry taken up by revolutionary communists and often wrongly attributed to Marx.

Mikhail Bakunin (1814–1876)
Russian anarchist leader who eventually came into conflict with Marx. He believed that communism was the first step towards anarchism.

Marx was influenced by many different philosophers, thinkers and social reformers, but the most important of them all was Hegel.

THE IMPORTANCE OF HEGEL
Hegel's philosophy is difficult to put into simple terms. It is often obscure and not related to the real world. His philosophical arguments have two main strands. The first is that human civilization comes about through intellectual and moral progress and that this is due to some kind of rational spirit that exists in humanity (universal mind) and not through divine intervention. The second is the development of the

dialectic – that is the idea that change comes about as a result of conflict between two opposing movements. He saw this development consisting of three stages.

* Thesis: the original idea.
* Antithesis: the second, contradictory viewpoint.
* Synthesis: the amalgamation of the two opposing views.

In Hegel's view, ideas develop through contradiction. The original idea or thesis is set up but is then contradicted and rejected by the antithesis. Eventually the best parts of both the thesis and antithesis can be combined, this is called the synthesis. Synthesis of ideas cannot take place until the first two stages are complete. Because the synthesis is made from the amalgamation of two opposing viewpoints it also must eventually be opposed or rejected. A new idea will then take its place,

to again be contradicted. To Hegel ideas were constantly developing and changing. This idea contrasted with the beliefs of the materialist philosophers who went before; they believed that everything followed immutable natural laws, seeing man as a cog in a machine that he could not influence.

Marx later took this idea of the dialectic and applied it in a practical way to the development of society and the economy instead of to the purely philosophical world of ideas. He showed that ideas developed from the material world of economics; in other words the conditions in which a person lives and works affect the way in which he thinks. This seems obvious to us today.

HOW DID MARX DIFFER FROM THOSE WHO WENT BEFORE?

Hegel's ideas were important, but Marx did not think they went far enough. Hegel believed that civilization had reached its final stage in the Prussian Empire and that there was no need for it to progress any further; he believed the state was the most important part of society. He accepted the political development and religious views within the Prussian Empire, so he believed that in any conflict between the state and the individual, the state should prevail. He also held the rather contradictory view that human consciousness could achieve self-understanding and freedom. It was these apparent contradictions that were discussed by the Young Hegelians, a group of philosophers led by Bruno Bauer, a lecturer, theologian and historian at the University of Berlin. Marx came into contact with them during his time at university and they were instrumental in shaping his philosophy.

Hegel said that people felt **alienated** from the world around them because of religious views that mean they are striving to live in an ideal world that they can only inhabit when they die. Bauer and Feuerbach also criticized religion and tried to show people that God was a creation of their own minds and that there was no need to feel alienated. Feuerbach felt

> **KEYWORD**
>
> Alienated: feeling isolated or estranged from society.

that even Hegel's concept of a 'universal mind' alienated people and that man himself was the centre of philosophy. He felt that the universal mind was a concept that prevented people from believing they could change their situation.

Where Marx differed from all these philosophers was in his realization that it was not 'God' or 'mind' that alienated people, but money. In *On the Jewish Question* 1844 Marx argues that: 'money is the alienated essence of man's labour and life … it dominates him as he worships it'. Marx decided to devote his life to the study of economics and the way in which it affected social develop-

> **KEYWORD**
>
> Dialectical materialism: Marxist way of studying the relationship between the real world and the world of ideas.

ment. He developed **dialectical materialism**, a means of studying the ways in which the material world affects the world of ideas.

THE INFLUENCE OF ENGELS

There is no doubt that Engels was an important figure to Marx. On completing *Das Kapital* in 1867 Marx wrote in a letter to Engels 'I owe it all to you, that this has been possible'. As the son of a wealthy manufacturer, Engels was able to support the Marx family financially, allowing Marx to continue with his research and writing. There is great academic debate over the part Engels played in formulating Marx's philosophy however. It is difficult for us to know now how much Engels actually contributed to the body of work Marx published during his lifetime.

Marx met Engels in Paris where they became great friends and co-writers and began collaborating on *The Holy Family* in 1845. This was intended to be a pamphlet exploring the class struggle but it eventually became a 300 page book. Engels only contributed 15 pages to the total. Other works on which they collaborated were *The German Ideology* (1845–1846), a criticism of the current German philosophy, and *The Communist Manifesto* (1848). Again, we know from documentary evidence that Marx contributed most of the writing.

It is alleged that Engels wrote newspaper articles on behalf of Marx when Marx was too busy to do his own research. He also helped with translation and as an interpreter when Marx met foreign worker's leaders. Engels wrote mainly about science, business, and industrial practice, of which he had first hand experience from his father's textile mill in Manchester, north England. He also specialized in writing on questions of war and nationalism.

It is well known that he completed the second and third volumes of *Das Kapital* from the unfinished manuscripts and notes that Marx left behind after his death. Marx was notorious for having bad handwriting and being badly organized, so it was fortunate that the business-minded and efficient Engels was available to sort everything out. How much he altered the original manuscripts, or put his own interpretation on the work, is open to speculation.

When Marx died, Engels became *the* well-known authority on communism and tried to keep all followers to the true path. He became the interpreter of all that Marx had said or written and kept up a huge correspondence until his own death in 1895.

---

* * * *SUMMARY* * * *

- Marx was both a philosopher and an economist, but he believed philosophy was not enough to change the course of the world.

- He studied philosophy as far back as the ancient Greeks.

- Philosophers at the time Marx was writing saw the world in either idealist or materialist terms.

- Marx's view was materialist and developed from the ideas of Hegel, Bauer and Feuerbach.

- His main contribution to the development of philosophy was dialectical materialism, a way of studying the relationship between the material world and the world of ideas.

- Fredrich Engels was an important figure in the life of Karl Marx, but academics cannot agree on the amount he contributed to Marx's philosophy.

3 Economic Theory

Marx's major work on economics was *Das Kapital*. In this he looks at the form the capitalist economy takes and explains his economic theories in great detail. The first nine chapters deal with the explanation of his economic theory, while the rest of the book explores the evidence that shows the ways in which capitalists exploit their workers. It is not an easy read, especially as many people today are not always aware of the literary references that he uses. It is also rather off-putting to open a book and find it seems to consist of 50 per cent footnotes in tiny writing! However, it is worth reading, and actually the footnotes are some of the most interesting bits. Fortunately, for those without the time for a marathon reading session, there are two other works that explain Marx's economic theory. As these were based on lectures given to working men's associations they are expressed in much simpler terms, but they still explain his economic theories in great detail. They are:

* *Wage Labour and Capital*: based on lectures given in 1847 and finally published in 1849;

* *Value, Price and Profit*: based on lectures given in 1865 and not discovered until after Marx's death.

THE CAPITALIST ECONOMY

Initially Marx described the capitalist system which he saw had developed in Europe from feudalism. Under the feudal system, workers were tied to plots of land without rights. Their **surplus products** then became the property of an aristocratic landlord class. The capitalist system had a different economic structure because it relied on costly machinery and factories before products could be made. Only those with money to invest could afford to own these. Capitalism was unique because:

* only under capitalism does human labour power become a **commodity** to be bought or sold;

* under capitalism all production is the production of commodities.

Under the feudal system, the landlord allowed his workers to cultivate the land in return for unpaid work, or rent, or both. It was obvious to all concerned that the landlord acquired the surplus product. Under capitalism this fact is hidden. Workers appear to be free to sell their labour power to the person who will give them the highest wages. It appears that they are given a fair day's wage for a day's work, but according to Marx they are being exploited. This exploitation is hidden by wages that allow the capitalist to cash in on the surplus produced by the workers. This is the **theory of surplus value** and it took Marx many years to work the theory out. It is a difficult concept,

> **KEYWORDS**
>
> Surplus products: products over and above those that satisfy the basic needs of the producers.
>
> Commodity: an object for use that is produced for sale and that can be valued in two different ways (see below).
>
> Theory of surplus value: Marxist theory that explains how capitalists are able to profit from their workers' labour power.

based on what a person's labour, or work, is actually worth and how it is exchanged for goods. To explain this it is necessary to go into detail about the way the capitalist economy works, and it is more easily understood by going back to the basics of the economy as Marx did, starting with the labour theory of value.

THE LABOUR THEORY OF VALUE

All products in capitalism are commodities. According to Marx commodities are valued in two different ways.

* **Use-value**: this means a commodity has a value of 'usefulness' that meets the needs of the consumer. For example, shoes protect your feet, sugar sweetens food, etc.

* **Exchange-value**: this refers to the relationship between the different values of different commodities, one commodity being equal to another amount of any other commodity. For example, a barrel of wine may be worth ten barrels of fish, fifty kilos of sugar, or ten pairs of shoes, etc.

Use-values are not dependent on markets or any other system of exchange, sugar will always be useful for its sweetness. Exchange-values are dependent on market forces. For example, a barrel of wine may be worth nine barrels of fish one week and 11 barrels of fish the following week. In order to understand how the capitalist makes a profit, Marx first of all had to understand and explain the rates at which goods are exchanged against each other. What is it about ten pairs of shoes that makes them worth a barrel of wine? Marx believed it was the amount of labour that went into making the product that determined the exchange-value.

Labour must be applied to any commodity to give it use-value. For example, to produce a barrel of fish someone needs to catch the fish, salt them and put them in a barrel, and to make shoes a cobbler would have to produce and work on a piece of leather. This is what

KEYWORD

Concrete labour: labour that has to be applied to a product to give it use-value.

Marx called **concrete labour**. Each different commodity needs a different amount of concrete labour applied to it. For example, it may take five hours to catch and salt a barrel of fish while it may take ten hours to make a pair of shoes.

Because the commodities need to be exchanged, they must have some kind of value in common, a way of working out what they are worth against each other. What they have in common is called their 'value' by Marx. The value is in the commodities because they are all products of human labour; therefore the exchange-value of the goods can be worked out from the amount of labour that has gone into making the finished product. If a cobbler spends ten hours making shoes and a fisherman takes five hours to collect a barrel of fish, then a fair rate of exchange would be two barrels of fish to one pair of shoes.

This is a very simple theory, which doesn't take into account the cost of raw materials, the difficulty of the job or the skill of the worker. For example, an apprentice cobbler may take 20 hours to make a pair of shoes but this does not make the shoes more valuable. The labour theory of value depends on how much labour on average it takes to make a product, or as Marx called it the 'socially necessary' labour time.

MONEY AND CAPITAL

In a capitalist economy, goods are not usually bartered or exchanged in this way. We use money to buy products from the shops or markets. Money represents the value of goods and is a useful means of exchange. Money existed

in societies that existed before capitalism, but not all money is **capital**. Capital is money that is taken into circulation in order to make more money. In Marxist terms, capital is money to which surplus value accrues. Marx puzzled over the way in which the capitalist was able to extract this surplus value: what is the means by which a capitalist makes a profit? If labour is a commodity then, like other commodities, it should be exchanged for its value. The capitalist who employs a worker for a day should pay on average the value of a day's labour which will add the cost of a day's labour, to the cost of producing the item. Following the exchange-value of labour theory, the capitalist can only sell or exchange the commodity at a rate of exchange corresponding to the value of the labour that was used to produce it. It would seem impossible for the capitalist to make a profit, so how does he do it? Marx worked out the solution to this problem which had puzzled many economists before him. The answer lies in the difference between labour and labour power.

LABOUR AND LABOUR POWER

Labour power is the muscle power, strength and skill which the capitalist has to buy from the worker in order to produce goods. It is a commodity with a value. If the value of a commodity is the amount of labour that goes into producing it, how much is labour power worth? Because labour power is the strength

KEYWORDS

Labour power: the strength and skills of the worker.

Labour: work done to add value to raw materials.

and skill of worker, then its value must be the value of the food, shelter, clothing, etc. that it takes to keep the worker in a fit condition to be able to work. **Labour** is the actual work that is done, the activity which adds value to raw materials.

When a capitalist hires a worker, his labour power becomes labour which belongs to the capitalist. The worker is paid for his labour power at an hourly rate but what he is actually being paid for is his labour. There is a difference between the value of the wage which the worker receives for his labour power and the value which is created by his labour. This is the surplus value that belongs to the capitalist.

SURPLUS VALUE

Finally we get to the explanation of Marx's discovery of how the capitalist makes a profit from his workers! The capitalist pays the worker for a day's labour power and gains wealth because the worker always gets a fixed amount for his labour power, regardless of the profit the capitalist makes. This is more easily understood by using an example.

If the cost of keeping a worker alive for a day is $1 and his working day is ten hours then the exchange value of ten hours, labour is $1. In a factory, a worker may be able to add $1 to the value of raw materials in eight hours. The worker has earned his wage in eight hours, but the capitalist has bought ten hours of labour power so he is able to make a profit from the last two hours of the worker's day. This profit, is of course, multiplied by the number of workers in the factory. In effect, the capitalist gets the use-value of the worker's labour power but pays only the exchange-value.

Marx saw that the working day was divided into two parts:

* **Necessary labour**: the time the worker spends actually earning the amount paid in wages. In any society a worker would need to labour for a period of time in order to provide the food, clothing and shelter he requires. The amount of time this takes will vary with the technology that is available to help him with his work.

* **Surplus labour**: the time spent producing surplus value for the capitalist.

The capitalist can increase his surplus value in two ways.

* By making the working day longer.

* By increasing efficiency in the workplace so the worker covers the cost of his wages in a shorter time. This means more of the rest of the day is available to produce surplus value.

PROFIT AND THE DIVISION OF LABOUR

The chief driving force in capitalism is profit. Not all the surplus value the capitalist gains from his workers is profit because he has had to pay for machinery, training, etc. The rate of profit the capitalist receives is variable and he is always looking for ways to improve it.

The capitalist system differs from past production methods by using a way of working called the division of labour. This is the use of mass production systems within the workplace so that a process is split into a number of repetitive tasks. For example, the cobbler takes a piece of leather through every process himself until he finishes a pair of shoes.

In a shoe factory, the work is done by machines in a number of different stages: one machine cuts the leather, one sews it, one shapes it, etc. This improves the capitalists profits because:

* one worker can do the work of several others. This will increase competition for jobs, so wages go down;

* it makes the work simple and unskilled so there is no need for long apprenticeships or training;

* small-scale capitalists are put out of business because they cannot compete with the low prices of the large-scale manufacturers. They then have to join the workers.

However, this increased profit can only be gained in the short term. Once the capitalist's more efficient and improved production methods have spread to other manufacturers there will be an abundance of his product on the market. This is known as over-production and competition in the marketplace will eventually reduce the price of his commodity.

The capitalist can solve his problem in the short term by:

* exploiting old markets more efficiently, for example, by advertising;
* opening up new markets, for example, exporting to other countries.

Marx noted that there is always a tendency for the rate of profit to fall. Increased competition is one of the main factors in this because the capitalist finds he has to invest increasing amounts of capital into his business.

CAPITALISM IN CRISIS

Marx believed that capitalism was in crisis and internal contradictions would eventually lead to its downfall. The main problems that Marx predicted were:

* workers' wages will tend to fall to subsistence level;
* profits will tend to fall;
* competition will lead to large companies swallowing up small ones; and this will be opposed by growing numbers of workers;
* more people will be forced into the working class;
* the capitalist system will lead to greater divisions in society;
* there will be more and more severe economic crises;
* capitalism will reduce workers to a degraded condition and these workers will eventually rise up in revolution and overthrow the system.

The only solution that Marx saw to these problems was the setting up of a communist society and this could only be the result of revolution. In capitalism, the price of goods, and the profits made, are dependent to a great extent on the markets and on wages. High wages for workers lead to high prices for commodities, therefore factory owners get low profits. Low wages for workers mean that they are unable to buy enough goods and services to keep the economy viable and this leads to unemployment.

Marx saw the competition between rival capitalists as one of the main economic problems and he believed that, in a communist society, the economy should be managed centrally.

* Important industries would be centralized; only useful goods and services would be produced and over-production would stop.
* Banks would be centralized; it is only in this way that society can be sure there would be high levels of investment in the right kind of industries.
* There would be controls on imports to help combat unemployment.

The predictions that Marx made about the economy have not all come about. Profits do not tend to fall, workers' wages have improved in real terms, and the majority of people are much better off than they were in Marx's day. For the majority of people in society, class divisions have become less. Where communists have come to power through revolutions their economies have suffered just as many economic crises as capitalist countries, although for different reasons. However, we have seen the takeover of smaller companies by large ones and several depressions in the economy with periods of high unemployment, so Marx wasn't totally wrong, and we can't predict exactly what will happen to the economy next.

Marx's economic theories were important because they made people look at a system that had become cruel and inhuman. He showed that the increase in productivity brought about by the Industrial Revolution did nothing to benefit working people. The quality of their lives was much worse than before.

Marx thought one of the major benefits to this inhuman society would be a shorter working day. In *Das Kapital* there is a whole chapter devoted to this subject, with harrowing descriptions of children being forced to work long hours, in one case for 36 hours. No wonder the average age of death among the working classes was 19 years in the Victorian era. In most democratic countries today there are laws to regulate the hours that people have to work. The workers who had to fight for improvements in working conditions by uniting against the capitalists found their inspiration in the works of Marx.

✱✱✱✱SUMMARY ✱✱✱✱

● Marx explained his economic theory in *Das Kapital*. It is also explained in *Wage Labour and Capital* and in *Value, Price and Profit*.

● The capitalist economy needs costly machinery to produce goods. Only those who can afford to invest capital can profit.

● All production under capitalism is the production of commodities. Human labour power becomes a commodity under capitalism.

● Marx believed workers are exploited by capitalists, but they are not aware of it.

● Commodities have two types of value: use-value and exchange-value.

● The rate at which commodities are exchanged against each other depends on the amount of labour that has gone into making them.

● In a capitalist society money is used as an indirect way of exchanging goods. Not all money is capital. Capital is money to which surplus value accrues.

● Capitalists gain surplus value from their workers by paying them a fixed amount for their labour power regardless of the profit they gain.

● Surplus value can be increased by lengthening the working day or increasing productivity.

● Not all surplus value is profit.

● Division of labour increases profit in the short term.

● Profits fall in the long term due to over-production and increased competition which leads to increasing investment.

● Marx believed capitalism was in crisis and this would eventually lead to revolution.

● Marx believed that in a communist society the economy should be managed centrally.

4 Economy and Society

For Marx, economics did not exist in a vacuum, as a subject to be studied for its own sake. He was interested in the way that the economic structure of society affected the lives of the people within it. The capitalist society had developed fairly gradually in Europe, but in the second half of the nineteenth century it had started to develop very rapidly and technological change was speeding up. Marx saw that this had very definite effects on the lives of everybody, rich and poor. He also saw that the effects of capitalist economy were starting to be felt around the world and not just in the countries that had developed their means of production.

FETISHISM

In primitive societies, and in some kinds of religion, inanimate objects are sometimes thought to have supernatural powers; for example, voodoo dolls or holy statues. In capitalist societies, people suffer from the illusion that money or commodities also have powers and properties of their own. A fetish is an

> **KEYWORD**
>
> Fetishism: desiring, worshipping or giving excessive concern to inanimate objects.

object of desire, worship or obsessive concern. Marx saw three types of **fetishism** in capitalist society:

* money;
* capital;
* commodities.

Money fetishism

Throughout history money has always had an element of fetishism about it, especially when it was in the form of precious metals, gold in particular. Seventeenth- and eighteenth-century European merchants were obsessed with gold and silver and believed that possession of large quantities of precious metals would be enough to enable a country to

win a war. However, gold in itself is worthless. For example, in the book *Treasure Island* by R.L. Stevenson the character Ben Gunn is marooned on a desert island with a treasure chest. The treaure is of no use to him because he cannot use it to buy anything with – what he really desires is a little bit of cheese! Money fetishism is an illusion that deceives workers, making them think of money as the goal of their labours and thinking of their worth in terms of money.

Capital fetishism

This is the belief that capital in itself is valuable and that it does not owe anything to the labour which goes to produce it. Marx argued capitalists felt that increased productivity was due to the capital they invested in their business and not the labour of the workers. Capitalists also feel that their money is productive when it is in a bank earning interest. Although it is making them a profit it is not actually producing anything.

Commodity fetishism

This is the belief that some commodities have a kind of intrinsic value that makes them more valuable than others and is not related to their exchange-value.

Marx believed that all three kinds of fetishism are features of capitalist society that stop people from understanding and changing the society. They are illusions that play a part in the alienation of humans under capitalism.

ALIENATION

Hegel had shown that people were alienated, but believed it was due to their yearning to be part of the 'universal mind'. Alienation for him was an almost religious concept. Marx saw alienation in practical economic terms. Workers are alienated from the products they make because they do not benefit from them. In *The German Ideology* of 1846 he wrote that workers saw the products of their labours as 'alien and outside them'. 'Labour produces fabulous things for the rich but misery for the poor' said Marx in *The Economic and Philosophic Manuscripts* of 1844.

Workers are alienated and depersonalized by the factory system because of the way in which the factory obtains surplus value from their labour. The factory system also means that they are told when to work, how to work and they derive very little personal satisfaction from their labours.

Alienation is connected to exploitation by the capitalist. The worker is not aware of the fact that he is being exploited. He believes the capitalist has a right to the surplus value that is produced because he believes that is just the way things are, or part of human nature.

Marx believed that capitalism seduces consumers by giving them desires that enslave them. The goods that a worker produces eventually enslave him because he is trapped in a cycle of working for money to buy goods; fetishism of goods means that people want to buy and consume more. The fetishism of money means that people have to sell themselves to obtain it and then desire money for its own sake. Private property also alienates people because they believe that an object only has worth if they can possess or use it.

Private property, wage labour, surplus value, and market forces are structures that have been constructed by people in society. These structures manipulate everyone in society but in subtle ways so they don't realize what is happening. Because people are not aware of the way in which they are manipulated by the economy they feel alienated and do not know why. Marx believed that even capitalists are alienated but, as he wrote in *The Holy Family* in 1846, they are 'happy in their alienation'. Their power, wealth and privilege is a substitute for true happiness.

On the other hand, the alienation of the workers is oppressive. They are the ones who truly suffer from alienation as they have nothing, neither the means of production nor the end products. All they hold is their labour power. The capitalist cannot exist without the worker; the worker believes he cannot survive without the capitalist because of the hold that money and wage labour have over him. In *The German Ideology* Marx describes how the abolition of private property and regulation of labour would abolish alienation between them and their products and would let them be in control of their lives again. Marx believed that realization of alienation was a vital step towards the revolution that would bring about communism.

CLASS AND CLASS STRUGGLE

Historians long before Marx had discovered the existence of classes. Marx did not define class in any of his works, and used the term rather loosely to mean different things at different times. He believed that class is defined

> **KEYWORD**
>
> Means of production: raw materials, factories, land that allow production to take place.

by economic factors. He saw that classes are made up of individuals who share a common relationship with the **means of production**. At the time he was writing he saw that the capitalist economy had divided society into two opposing camps: 'Two great classes opposing each other: Bourgeoisie and Proletariat' (*The Communist Manifesto*). Those that owned the means of production were the bourgeoisie, those that owned no means of production were the proletariat.

In the nineteenth century, everybody took the class structure for granted, as if it had always existed in its current form. Marx believed that classes had never existed in exactly that way before because the economic structure of society had not existed in a capitalist form before. He believed that class structure had actually become much simpler than it had been before and it was the needs of the capitalist system that had actually brought the working class into existence. The capitalist system needed wage labourers to survive, but in creating this class it had actually sown the seeds of its own destruction.

The aim of the bourgeoisie, or capitalist class, was to increase their profits by any means possible. The aim of the proletariat, or workers, was to improve their living and working conditions. Marx believed these needs were obviously in conflict and would lead to class struggle and ultimately to revolution. Class struggle does not necessarily mean violent struggle, although Marx did believe that this would occur. Class struggle can be any social action that results from the different interests of classes, for example, demonstrating or writing a letter of protest.

In Marxist theory it is seen as necessary to allow class consciousness to develop. Marx talked of a class 'in itself' and a class 'for itself'. A class 'in itself' refers to a group of individuals who share the same relationship to the means of production and share common interests. A class 'for itself' is a class that is conscious of these interests; a class that has discovered that it is alienated. The way for workers to realize they are alienated is through education and by political means. He thought that the workers were the only class in society who could achieve a new form of society, a communist society.

THE COMMUNIST MANIFESTO AND CLASS STRUGGLE

The **manifesto** of the Communist Party was written by Marx and Engels in 1848 as a platform for the Communist League, a working men's association. The Communist League had developed out of the League of the Just, and

KEYWORD

Manifesto: official statement of political intent.

originally it consisted of only German members. At first it contained numerous anarchists whose idea was to destroy the factory system by violent means and return to an agricultural and small-craft society. Marx and Engels took on the task of reorganizing the Communist League. There were numerous disagreements with the anarchists, who eventually formed their own societies. Marx believed it was important for the ideas of the Communist League to be spread around the world and eventually *The Communist Manifesto* was translated into many languages.

The beginning of *The Communist Manifesto* describes the rise of the capitalist system and the class differences between the proletariat and the bourgeoisie. Marx then describes the future of the class struggle and its importance to the liberation of the worker.

He describes how dissatisfaction with working conditions and poor wages mean that workers club together to form trade unions, to keep up the rates of wages and to plan revolts against capitalist domination. He notes that sometimes the revolts will turn into violent riots which, though successful locally, do not benefit the proletariat as a class. The benefit of these revolts is not in the result of the action taken, but in the way in which the workers have grouped together to form unions.

Marx thought unions would keep expanding and this would be helped by modern forms of communication like the railways. Contacts among groups could be made and eventually the numerous local struggles could be centralized to become a national struggle between the classes. Eventually an international struggle would take place.

The proletariat need to become better organized and to stop any in-fighting between different factions. This will make them stronger and able to take advantage of divisions among the bourgeoisie. Eventually a revolution will occur, for only a revolution can overthrow a system that is spreading its tentacles all over the world.

IMPERIALISM AND COLONIALISM

KEYWORD

Imperialism: economic and political domination of one society by another.

Marx believed profits under capitalism would fall and that one short-term way of slowing down the rate at which they fell was by opening up new markets. This meant the capitalists had to export their goods into other countries. When Marx was developing these economic theories, British **imperialism** meant there was a huge overseas market for mass produced goods: the British Empire.

Historians divide imperialism into periods of time or epochs.

✳ **Mercantile capitalism:** this is the first stage of imperialism. It began in the sixteenth century when explorers discovered new continents and plundered them. Large companies became the governing power in countries where they settled.

✳ **Colonialism:** this is the second stage of imperialism. Capitalist countries took over governing power from the companies set up under mercantile capitalism. Where the local population would not accept this rule they used armed force.

Colonialism meant there were excellent protected markets for manufactured goods from Europe. These were often developed at the expense of the local industries. Historians believe millions of villagers died of starvation in India because their traditional textile industry was ruined by imports of cheap manufactured cotton from Lancashire. India and other countries were turned into suppliers of cheap raw materials for British industry.

Capitalism was prevented from developing in these countries in the early stages of colonialism. It was only later, at the beginning of the twentieth century, that the capitalist system itself began to be exported. There was investment in the employment of industrial workers in the colonies, but only when this did not

KEYWORD

Third world: poor, less industrialized and under-developed countries, often former colonies.

interfere with industries in Britain and the other imperialist states. This was mainly in industries that were fairly close to the raw materials: mining, food processing, etc. Some modern Marxists believe this led the way to development of the **third world** and the current stage of imperialism, neo-colonialism.

Marx believed that these stages were necessary if the revolution was to take place on a worldwide scale. He was convinced that revolution could only take place if societies had developed to the stage of capitalism with the class divisions of bourgeoisie and proletariat. It was the proletariat who would start the revolution. The revolutionary process would have two stages.

* A bourgeois revolution against imperialism.

* A revolution of the proletariat against the bourgeoisie.

Marx saw the world economic situation in a rather simple way. Each colony had very different social structures and, although world capitalism did develop, it was combined with other economic systems in many countries. Where revolution did occur in these countries, the words of Marx were often distorted to fit the requirements of anybody who wished to see a change in the political system in their country. A truly communist society was never the result.

* * * *SUMMARY* * * *

• Marx was interested in the ways in which the economy affected society.

• He described how fetishism of money, capital and commodities alienated people.

• Alienation is connected to exploitation. People are alienated by a society which they have constructed but they don't realize this.

• Workers are oppressed by their alienation because they do not own the means of production.

• Capitalist are alienated but are happy in the alienation because they have material possessions.

• The class structure became simpler under capitalism, creating the bourgeoisie and proletariat.

• Class struggle occurs when workers realize they are alienated.

• Class struggle leads to revolution and a fairer communist society.

• Marx and Engels wrote *The Communist Manifesto*. It describes the development of capitalism, the class struggle and the need for revolution.

• Workers need to unite together in order to overthrow the capitalist system.

• Capitalism spread around the world through imperialism.

• Communism could also spread around the world, but colonies would only be ready for revolution after industrialization had taken place.

History, Society and Revolution

5

Marx spent many years studying the development of the capitalist system that had grown up in Europe after the Industrial Revolution. He believed a scientific study of the ways in which society had developed would help prepare the working classes to overthrow the system by showing them the historical perspective of their position. He believed that capitalism was the latest form of exploitation in a series of oppressive rules throughout history, and that if people were shown this then they could be persuaded to take action against their oppressors.

His study of the development of society was concerned with two main strands:

* the development of the economy;
* the dialectical view of history.

THE DEVELOPMENT OF THE CAPITALIST ECONOMY

In the earliest societies, when people lived as hunter-gatherers and small-scale farmers, there were no real classes as society was organized on the basis of common labour and mutual protection; there was no private property. People scratched out an existence at subsistence level and had just enough food for basic survival. In Marxist theory this type of society is known as 'primitive communism'.

As societies became more efficient in producing food, the surplus products often came under the control of a ruling elite. This elite was often only a minority of the society as a whole. Throughout history the ruling elite has changed, examples are: slave owners, religious leaders of many types, feudal lords and, finally, capitalists.

In *The Communist Manifesto*, Marx and Engels defined capitalists as the owners of the means of production and the employers of wage labourers. Because the factory system that sprang up after the Industrial Revolution was based on the purchase of large items of machinery, it was only a minority of the population who could afford to invest in it, so they became the new ruling elite.

THE DIALECTICAL VIEW OF HISTORY AND SOCIETY

Marx saw history as a series of dialectical conflicts. Each type of society, whether based on slavery, feudalism, or capitalism, contains contradictions inside its structure which can only be expressed through conflict. These conflicts will eventually lead to the downfall of the system. A new system will then take its place. Marx said this had been demonstrated throughout history.

In the original hunter-gatherer societies there was no real division of labour: everybody could do any job that needed to be done, and could use any of the tools that were available. These societies were classless, in a Marxist sense, but then they developed into slave-owning societies which became unstable and collapsed due to internal contradictions. The ownership of slaves was dependent on warfare which put pressure on the economy. Eventually this undermined the power of the state, allowing barbarian invasion, which led to the collapse of the system.

Feudalism replaced slavery in Europe and it allowed people to develop skills and talents under the patronage of the landed nobility. However, feudalism was eventually overthrown by revolutionary struggles which continued into the nineteenth century when the rise of capitalism began.

Capitalism was necessary to allow the development of the factory system and mass production. People had to be legally free to move to where the work was, instead of being tied to the land. The landowners also had to be legally free to accumulate wealth and to be able to invest it to make a profit.

According to Marx every social system has appeared not accidentally, but when it was historically necessary. Each new system outlives its usefulness. Within every process internal contradictions take place that bring down the system. Nothing can remain stable, as the social structure is dependent on the economic structure. This is the basic premise of dialectical materialism.

Marx believed that the key to understanding the history of human society was exploitation. To Marx, class divisions were not simply between rich and poor. Classes were defined by how people stood in relation to the means of production. Those who produced food, clothing, shelter and so on have always been exploited. The surplus products they made were always controlled by a class of non-producers except in very primitive societies. For example, in feudal societies everyone had to give a tenth of their produce (a tithe) to the Church.

To Marx, the history of the world was the history of class warfare. Classes must always be in competition with those that are above or below them. He believed the course of history was economically determined and capitalism could only end in revolution.

IS REVOLUTION INEVITABLE?

Marx saw revolution as a good thing and not to be avoided. The conclusion he drew from his dialectical study of society was that it was not only desirable, but inevitable, because of the internal conflicts inherent in capitalism. In *The Communist Manifesto* he describes how capitalism has divided society into two opposing camps.

* **Proletariat**: workers who have no capital or means of production of their own. They are reduced to selling their labour power in order to live.

* **Bourgeoisie**: the class of capitalists. Owners of the means of production and employers of wage labourers.

According to Marx, these polar opposites could not exist together in a stable society. Dialectical theory means that the proletariat must overthrow the bourgeoisie. 'The history of all hitherto existing societies has been the history of class struggle' he argues in *The Communist Manifesto*. He believed that a better society could then be built, based on the principles of communism.

Marx was not the first to believe that society
should be improved. Many of his ideas were
developed from those of the **utopian socialists**, such as Robert Owen and Charles Fourier.
They had criticized the capitalist system and
shown how inhumane and oppressive it was.
They believed in a socialist society where there

KEYWORDS

Utopian socialists: believers
in a mythical, perfect state.

Philanthropy: practical
benevolence.

was common ownership of the means of production. Where Marx
differed from them was in the method he believed would bring about
this society. The utopians believed reason was the best way to bring
about a change in the views of society. They set up model communities
and factories where hours were regulated, workers were treated fairly
and given access to education, good homes and nourishing food. They
believed these examples of **philanthropy** would be enough to bring
about change in society.

Marx agreed with the humanitarian changes that were made, but
thought that good housing, medical care, education and wage reforms
did not get to the root of the problem, which was the exploitation of
one class by another. If the economic base of society is the real source
of the conflicts within it, no amount of workers' benefits will resolve
the problem. The contradictions within the capitalist system will
continue to accumulate. Change will only come about when workers
take over factories, mines and banks by force. 'The weapon of criticism
obviously cannot replace the criticism of weapons. Material force must
be overthrown by material force.' In other words if people use force
against you, you must use it back.

Another reason Marx believed in the inevitability of revolution was his
view of the state. He was the first to realize that 'the state' is not an
impartial body that works for the benefit of everybody in society. Most
materialist philosophers, including Hegel, viewed the state as a part of
the natural order which was necessary to the working of society. Marx
believed the state exists to protect the ruling class and suppress those
that produce wealth for them. For example, in feudal societies laws were

made in favour of the land-owning classes. Trespassing or poaching were often punished severely, even by death. In a capitalist society, laws are passed that curb the power of trade unions and the media are controlled by the rich who can use them to attack anyone who upsets the status quo. These factors make it even more likely that revolution must take place against the vested interests in capitalism. The state will try to block any changes that undermine its powers of suppression.

Marx believed that revolution would:

* begin in the industrialized capitalist countries of Europe, such as Britain and Prussia;

* spread rapidly around the rest of the world because of the way in which countries had become economically dependent on each other.

Time has proved him wrong on both these points. The first communist revolution was in Russia, a country based on a peasant economy. It remained the only communist country for nearly 30 years.

As a philosopher, Marx saw benefits to the individual from revolution. In a *Contribution to the Critique of Hegel's Philosophy in Right* (1849) Marx claims that: 'In a revolution to change society men change themselves.' This is because he believed that people were not really free when they were subject to forces they couldn't understand. He hoped his writings would help them to realize these forces existed and that they were the products of the human mind. The human mind, not a god or universal mind, had created the economy and social structure that oppressed them. When people realized this they would be free to take responsibility for their own actions and change both themselves and the world.

AFTER THE REVOLUTION

Marx did not write a great deal about the form that society would take after the revolution, or how it would be organized. He believed society would eventually be stateless because he believed the state was a tool

that let one branch of society oppress another. After the revolution the state would 'wither away' as there would be no oppression. Because he believed the ownership of property defines the class system, it was important to Marx that private property should be abolished. This would mean that classes would eventually cease to exist, so there would be no inequality and no need for further class struggle. He also thought that when the means of production were centralized, private property would disappear and money would then cease to exist.

Marx did not believe that it would be possible to go directly from a capitalist society to a communist one. There would have to be an intermediate stage between the two known as **socialism**. Under socialism there would be a **dictatorship of the proletariat** and the communist party would have to act as the **vanguard of the proletariat**. This is because the majority of the population will still be victims of alienation and false consciousness and must be led to a true understanding of communism.

This is a useful concept for dictators who wish to impose an undemocratic rule in the name of Marx. It was a theory that was developed by Vladimir Ilyich Lenin (1870–1924), a Russian communist leader, at the start of the first communist revolution.

KEYWORDS

Socialism: in Marxist theory the stage between revolution and true communism.

Dictatorship of the proletariat: unavoidable undemocratic state made necessary after communist revolution.

Vanguard of the proletariat: leaders of the communist movement who aim to educate the proletariat.

Today the word 'socialism' has become a much less easily defined term, referring to any system where there is state control, planning, and ownership of the means of production. It also encompasses some element of social care for the sick, children, the elderly and those in extreme poverty. Many would argue that those countries that declare themselves to be communist states are actually only at the state of socialism.

COMMUNIST SOCIETY

The main writings we have on the form that a communist society would take are *The Principles of Communism* written by Engels in 1847. These set out the views of the Communist League, of which Marx was a member. These are the main points of the document.

* Limitation of private property through progressive taxation, inheritance tax and abolition of inheritance rights for the family.

* Capitalists to be expropriated through competition with state industry and partial compensation.

* Confiscation of the possessions of emigrants and rebels against the majority.

* Central organization of wages for workers on the land, or in factories. Competition between workers to be abolished.

* All members of society to be equally liable for work until private property is abolished. Industrial armies to be formed, especially for agriculture.

* Private banks to be suppressed and money and credit to be centralized in national banks.

* State-owned factories, workshops etc., to be developed as far as economically feasible; agriculture to be improved.

* Education for all children at state schools, paid for by the state.

* Communal dwellings to be built on waste land to combine the best of rural and urban life.

* Insanitary housing to be destroyed.

* Equal inheritance rights for children born out of wedlock.

* Transport to be nationalized.

It was not considered feasible that all these changes could take place at once. It was felt that once one change would made others would follow and they would accumulate.

✳ ✳ ✳ ✳ SUMMARY ✳ ✳ ✳ ✳

• Marx spent years refining his theories on the dialectical view of history and the development of the economy.

• He believed that society was always dominated by a ruling elite that controlled the means of production and the surplus products of the workers.

• He saw the history of society as a series of dialectical conflicts. Societies were continually destroyed by internal contradictions and then replaced.

• The capitalist system was the latest form of exploitation in a series of oppressive systems through history.

• The state is not an independent body but a tool that capitalists use to oppress the workers.

• Because the proletariat and bourgeoisie could not exist together in a stable society revolution would be inevitable.

• Society after the revolution would be communist. The means of production would be centralized. Private property would be abolished and money would cease to exist.

• Before a communist state existed an intermediate socialist state would exist which may have to use undemocratic methods such as the dictatorship of the proletariat.

Further Marxist Thought

6

Marx wrote a great deal about society and the economy and the way in which the relationship between them had developed throughout history. He looked at the world in a new way and shed new light on the relationship between individuals and the society in which they live in. At the time he was writing his ideas were considered extremely radical, but today we take many of them for granted, for example, equal rights for men, women and children.

IDEOLOGY

According to Marx, each society is unique and has its own **ideology** – each society has its own assumptions about the nature of humanity and has its own morality and values. At the time that Marx was writing most philosopers believed ideas and consciousness were the shaping force of world history. Marx maintained, in his materialist view, that the way people thought was a

> # KEYWORDS
>
> Ideology: world view; the perception people have of the world around them.
>
> Economic base: the way the economy is structured in a society.

reflection of the **economic base** of the country in which they lived. Social consciousness – people's ideas, assumptions and ways of thinking – reflected the society in which they lived, so society was shaped by the modes of production prevalent at that time. He believed the same economic base would sustain many different kinds of society depending on historical and political factors. Even two fairly similar capitalist countries will have different social values. For example, although Britain, France and Germany are all capitalist countries in Europe, they have very different cultures.

Marx believed that the contradictions in the economic base were the driving force in historical struggle. He was not content to generalize on this point and spent a great many years of his life researching and analyzing political and ideological data on class struggles in the histories of many countries.

Marx believed that the ideas that rule any country, and the laws that develop from them, must be the ideas of the ruling class. These rules naturally develop from the society as it changes. They are not worked out in advance. When feudalism developed into capitalism, nobody sat down and worked out that they would need a population that was free to move around the country to find work instead of being tied to the land. It was just that the new necessities of life meant that society had to develop in the way that it did. People had to take risks and work out solutions to the new problems that the new economic structure posed.

Because the way that people actually think is influenced by the society around them, and the society that went before, they find it difficult to develop entirely new ideas. They can only think in the way that their language and concepts handed down to them allow. When people can-

> **KEYWORD**
>
> False consciousness: false beliefs or values created by a culture or society.

not see the way their beliefs are artificially constructed by society it is known in Marxist terms as **false consciousness**.

Most people tend to believe that the world that is around them is in a finished, fixed form that cannot be changed. They do not examine the way in which the society around them came about or what processes it went through to get there. This makes it difficult for them to envisage any kind of change to the system. At the time Marx was writing the divisions between the capitalist and the worker were seen as part of human nature and the natural order of society. This was reinforced by the fact that the capitalists control information, education and entertainment. For example, hymns in church spoke of 'the rich man in his castle, the poor man at his gate, God made them high or lowly and ordered their estate'. Marx believed that the only way to counteract this was with a revolutionary workers' party which would educate the workers so that they understood the ways in which they were being exploited and help them to revolt against it. Today we are much more aware of the conditioning of society and media manipulation, but only because Marx brought attention to the problem over a hundred years ago.

RELIGION

'Religion is the opium of the people' is one of Marx's most famous quotations. Opium is a drug that dulls the senses; Marx believed that religion had a similar function.

Marx had seen some of the problems that religion caused to his own family when his father renounced his Jewish faith. Prussia was an anti-Semitic country and Jews were not allowed to hold public office. Marx himself was an atheist and was greatly influenced by materialist philosophers and freethinkers such as David Hume (1711–1776) and Denis Diderot (1713–1784) who had concentrated on finding rational arguments against religion. Believers in scientific order and rationalism, they thought they could prove by scientific means that God could not exist. They thought that most people had a superstitious belief in God that would disappear when they were enlightened by the powers of reason.

Marx agreed with these rationalist philosophers to some extent. He was greatly influenced by Feuerbach, who said the essence of Christianity was the essence of mankind itself. Marx believed that God was created by human consciousness and was a product of human minds, but he wanted to understand *why* people worshipped God and why their religious beliefs took the form that they did. Again he spent many years researching and analyzing societies past and present, this time exploring the question of religion.

Eventually he came to the conclusion that religion is part of the ideological make-up of society. In primitive societies where people lives are dependent on their relationship with the natural world religion helps to unite them with nature. Natural forces are worshipped as gods and the natural cycles of their world become part of the religion. In more developed societies people become freed from their dependence on nature by use of technology, but they feel alienated from the society because they have little control over their daily lives. People then use religion as a means of expressing their frustrations.

Marx believed that any fulfilment people achieved from religion was illusory because religion is just another form of alienation. People do not realize they are not free and until they do they cannot change society. There is therefore little to be achieved by demonstrating a lack of science and reason in religion. Religion will only cease to exist when certain classes are no longer oppressed and everybody becomes equal. In the *Contribution to the Critique of Hegel's Philosophy* of 1844, he wrote that: 'The abolition of religion, as the illusory happiness of men, is a demand for their real happiness. The call to abandon their illusions about their condition is a call to abandon a condition which requires illusions.'

WOMEN'S RIGHTS AND THE FAMILY

In *The Communist Manifesto*, Marx and Engels take great pains to point out that the communists are not about to introduce 'a community of women' and break up the family. They had been accused of this in the press several times throughout the year of its publication, 1848. At that time women in most capitalist countries did not have the vote and, in the eyes of the law, they were seen as possessions belonging to their husbands.

Marx wanted everybody to be equal, men, women and children; he believed that a communist society without private property would ensure this. He felt that relations between the sexes and relations between parents and children were corrupted by wage labour and private property. In *The Communist Manifesto* he wrote: 'All family ties between the proletariat are torn asunder, children transformed into simple articles of commerce and instruments of labour.'

Class divisions at that time meant that men, women and children from the working class laboured for long hours in factories and mines. They had few opportunities for health care or education. Women in the middle classes did not work outside the home after marriage and it was not always seen as necessary to educate girls. Engels said: 'The modern individual family is based on the open or disguised enslavement of the woman.' This was written in *The Origin of the Family, Private Property and the State* of 1884, and based on extensive notes made by Marx shortly before he died. Marx believed that marriage could never be an equal partnership when women were treated as second-class citizens and men were seen as the head of the household, for this stopped women from reaching their true potential as individuals.

In an ideal communist society, Marx believed there would be equal access for all to work and education. Adequate childcare facilities would mean that women would no longer have to be financially dependent on their husbands. They would not be financially disadvantaged by bearing children and caring for them. Marx believed that bringing all women into the workplace was the first step into giving them equality. It would be the first step in getting them involved in planning the economy and so changing society. It would also be the first step in abolishing prostitution, which he saw as a by-product of a capitalist system that viewed everything in financial terms.

Marx always thought that it was not enough just to pass liberal laws giving rights to minorities if the whole structure of society and the economy remains the same. Laws can be passed to give rights to women, but it is only when the ideology of the society changes, so that women do not bear the entire burden of caring for the young and elderly, that women will be emancipated. This proved to be correct in many so-called communist societies, where women did a day's work, often in physically demanding jobs, but found that it was still their job to do the housework and the shopping. Not so very different from capitalist society!

ART AND CULTURE
Marx believed art and culture was an important part of any society. He believed an appreciation of art is vital for everybody in the society, for it helps us all to understand our society and also ourselves. He was very fond of using quotations from Greek literature and Shakespeare in his work – indeed *Das Kapital* is full of such references. This made it difficult for ordinary working people to understand Marx's work, and most

preferred to read Engels, who wrote in a more straightforward manner. (Of course many workers at that time could not read at all because they were not educated.)

Marx believed that art had become something reserved for an elite minority. In a capitalist system it is selected by a minority. The freedom to enjoy art is at the expense of those who work to produce the wealth that gives the minority the money and leisure time to enjoy art. Artists have to supply art that will satisfy the requirements and taste of this minority.

Marx went on to argue that capitalist society tends to see everything in financial terms. Everything is given a financial 'value'. Freedom of expression, craftsmanship, making things for their own sake become subordinated by time and money.

Marx believed that art, like society, developed as a series of dialectical contradictions. As members of a society, artists, writers and musicians must also be influenced by the prevailing ideology. There will always be a few who struggle to express themselves in new ways, contradicting the old forms of artistic expression. In this way art can subvert the bourgeois prejudices that prevail in a capitalist society.

Marx's view was that in the ideal communist society everyone will have access to the cultural heritage of society and artistic activities will stop being the preserve of a privileged minority.

FREEDOM AND THE INDIVIDUAL

Marx saw individuals as products of the society to which they belong. Each society has its own view on individuality because each society has its own ideology. Every different social system will place a different emphasis on the relationship between the individual and the society. In certain societies (for example, capitalist societies), the rights of the individual are highly prized. In other societies, the rights of the group are seen as more important than the rights of the individual.

Marx wrote of the alienation in the capitalist system that lead to competitive struggle between individuals. He felt this was a necessary stage on the way to communism where people find their true individuality without the need for destructive competitiveness. Because Marx believed it was the capitalist work system that stopped the individual reaching his true potential he felt only the rise of the proletariat and the change to a communist society would allow the individual his full rights. In the proposed communist society:

* labour would be centrally planned for producing the means of life according to agreed needs of the population as a whole;

* labour time would be reduced to increase free time for everyone. This would lead to artistic and scientific development for all and greater self-knowledge.

At the time Marx was writing, workers' groups were fighting for the essential rights of freedom.

* Freedom of speech.
* Freedom of assembly.
* Freedom of the press.
* Equality under the law.
* Equal rights to vote.

Marx did not disagree with any of these rights, but he believed that as long as the economic base of society was still capitalist then people were not free even if they had the rights by law. For example, although in the eyes of the law everybody is equal, those who are better off can afford better representation in court; there may be freedom of the press but only the very rich can afford to own a major newspaper. It is only when capitalism is overthrown by revolution that true freedom will occur.

✳ ✳ ✳ ✳*SUMMARY* ✳ ✳ ✳ ✳

- Each society has an ideology developed from its economic base.

- The way people think is influenced by the society around them.

- When people cannot see these influences it is known as false consciousness.

- False consciousness can be counteracted by education.

- Religion is the opium of the people. It helps people to overcome their feelings of alienation and to express their frustrations but the support it gives is illusory.

- Everyone in society should have equal rights. Women should not be excluded from the workplace because they care for children and the elderly.

- Art and culture are important because they allow people to understand the society in which they live.

- In a capitalist society art and culture are a minority interest for the elite.

- Capitalism puts a monetary value on everything, even artistic expression.

- Art can be used to subvert the ideology of a society.

- Individuality is a concept that changes with the ideology of a society.

- In a capitalist system individuality is important but alienation means that people are not free.

- All the above injustices could only be remedied in a communist system. People may be given rights under a capitalist system but until the structure of society is changed the advantages they gain are not true rights.

7 Marxism after Marx

Karl Marx died in 1883 but his work carried on. Engels continued writing *Das Kapital* and the philosophy of communism that they had developed together began to spread around the world, mainly through the labour movement and working men's groups.

In addition to his few books, Marx wrote numerous articles, pamphlets and speeches, many of which were not published until after his death. Because of the vast body of his work and its complexity it is easy for people to interpret his ideas in their own way and claim that their interpretation is the 'true' meaning of Marxism. In some ways it is similar to interpretations of the Bible – there are many kinds of churches that call themselves Christian but they all have their own ways of worshipping God and many believe that their way is the 'right' way. Many different regimes call themselves Marxist or communist but they do not necessarily have similar ideologies or political systems. In fact they may well have very little in common with the original ideas of Marx except for the use of his name. Marx became so upset by the many misinterpretations of his ideas that he is reported to have said, 'all I know is that I am not a Marxist'.

Many countries have declared themselves as communist, Marxist or socialist during the twentieth century. Some after one revolution, some after successive coups and revolutions, and some after no revolution at all. Each one of these countries could have several books written about them. It is not possible in a short chapter to go into detail about every communist state in the world and its relationship to the works of Marx. However, we can look at some of the ways in which Marx has influenced the modern world and see where his philosophy is relevant today.

From the widely differing versions of communism that developed after Marx's death there emerged two main strands.

Evolutionary communists

They believe in the power of the evolution of society. Communism will come about through the natural progress of society and the disintegration of the capitalist system due to its internal flaws. Evolutionary communists resemble utopian socialists to some extent in their belief that society can be changed for the better without revolution.

Revolutionary communists

They believe in the power of revolution in society. Communism will come about only through the overthrow of the bourgeoisie by violent means, including **terrorism**. Terrorists do not necessarily believe the state can be defeated by their actions, but hope to destroy the morale of the people and their support for

KEYWORD

Terrorism: the use of violence to make people accept radical social and political change.

the government. Marx himself believed in the power of revolution but thought that it should not be forced upon a populace that was unready. He had several vociferous arguments with the anarchist movement over this point.

RUSSIAN COMMUNISM

Russia was the first communist country in the world. The type of communism that evolved there had little in common with the type of society that Marx thought would develop after the revolution. However, because it was the first communist country and the only communist country for many years, people often believe that Russian communism is 'true communism'. They think that many of the wrongs which have taken place there are attributable to Marx and not to the interpretation of his words by others.

The first revolutionary communists were the **Bolsheviks** in Russia, led by Lenin. They overthrew the Romanov dynasty who had ruled the country in a feudal manner for 300 years. The communist uprising of 1917 came

as a surprise to most of the world who had
never heard of communism or Karl Marx.

Marx predicted that revolution would be start-
ed by the industrial working class or proletariat.
This class hardly existed at all in Russia in 1917.
It seems curious that the first communist revo-

lution took place in a country which had a large peasant population – at
least 80 per cent of the population as a whole.

The Russian Empire at that time was vast and, compared with much of
Europe, it was very backward and had little industrialization. Three-
quarters of the people lived off the land and barely subsisted through
the harsh winters. Although feudalism had been officially abolished in
1861, the serfs had to pay compensation to their landlords and were
worse off than before.

At the time of the revolution, Russia was ruled by the autocratic leader
Tsar Nicholas II (1868–1918) who had nominated friends and family to
the State Council, the chief governing body. It was obvious to outsiders
that the state was corrupt but it was not obvious that a revolution
would take place. Although country landlords had been made poor,
they were passive and the peasants were loyal to the Tsar. The urban
working class were a very small part of the population and were badly
organized. Although the government was inefficient, it was ruthless in
repressing any signs of anti-government activity. The press was
censored and dissidents were sent to live as outcasts in the harsh terrain
of Siberia, traditions that the communists followed when they came
into power.

Marxism came to Russia through the work of Georgi Plekhanov, son of
a landowner who moved to Europe. He was the first native Russian to
write about Marxism as it applied to his home country. His ideas were
carried by students to factories and towns and one of his chief converts
was Vladimir Ilyich Ulyanov, later to be known as Lenin. Lenin was

sent to Siberia for three years for preaching the words of Marx to factory workers. He became a ruthless leader of the people who took advantage of the chaos in his country to take power. Although Lenin was a charismatic leader it was not just his interpretation of Marx that led to revolution. It was a war that Marx could not have foreseen that became the catalyst for revolution and led to the first communist state.

Russia was already ravaged by industrial unrest and social dissatisfaction when World War I began, and initial patriotism turned into discontent, especially as many lives and areas of land were lost. Refugees caused a housing crisis, people were starving and prices were rising. The population became demoralized and war-weary. Lenin realized that peace was important to the population and insisted that the war would only end if capitalism was over-

KEYWORDS

Soviets: regionally elected local councils in communist Russia.

Nationalized: brought under state ownership.

Stalin (1879–1953): Russian peasant who became dictator.

thrown. He called for the peasants to redistribute the land and for political power to be held by the **soviets**. The Bolsheviks took power in October 1917 and declared a decree on peace. Lenin inaugurated the dictatorship of the proletariat to justify the role of the communist party, which did not have the complete support of the population. He believed it was important to create a true 'Socialist Man' who was free from the false consciousness that alienated him.

The communists hoped that spontaneous revolutions would take place throughout Europe, following the example of Russia, but they never materialized. Russia was the only socialist state in Europe for some time. After many years of civil war in Russia, a so-called communist state eventually evolved which had very little to do with the society envisaged by Marx and Engels. Free enterprise was abolished; land, banks, foreign trade and shipping were **nationalized**. This should have been the start of the ideal communist state in which Marx had believed, but Russia was really not developed enough economically for true communism to exist. The civil war that ravaged Russia after the revolution left the economy in ruins and the idealist leaders of the first revolution were eventually replaced, or died, some in suspicious circumstances. Josef **Stalin** became the virtual dictator after Lenin's death and the state that should have 'withered away' became all-powerful.

Stalin had to make Russia economically viable. To this end he pushed through several disastrous policies, which were intended to bring the very backward peasant economy in line with the major capitalist nations:

Collectivization of agriculture

Because agricultural production was inefficient, farmers were forced to join together in collectives and to work the land in common. The state set the targets for production, set the price for the crops and bought up any surplus products. In theory this should have worked, but in practice it failed because machinery and transport were inadequate. The farms were then inefficient. The state quota of the surplus product was set far too high so that peasants and animals starved, and there was often not enough seed to sow for the next year. This is one indication of how difficult it is to put Marxist theory into practice, especially in a country that has not attained the level of development Marx believed would be attained before revolution took place.

Forced industrialization

Stalin wanted to transform Russia from an agricultural society into an industrial one. He intended to do this by planning all industrial production from the centre. Production targets dominated political and economic life. Five-year plans were implemented with set targets to be reached by the end of the allotted time. In industrial terms the plan worked and the aims were achieved. Russian industry developed rapidly; in ten years it was level with that of the capitalist countries that had taken nearly two centuries to reach the same level. In human terms it led to great hardship for the people and a decrease in consumption that eventually depressed the economy. Again this shows how difficult it is to put theory into practice, especially under the wrong conditions.

Purges

Stalin wanted absolute power and the state became his tool. He used the army and the secret police to wipe out dissidents. Thousands were forced to take part in show trials as enemies of the people and were sentenced to life in labour camps or mental hospitals. Stalin wanted to bring Russia into the modern world and was prepared to inflict suffering on the people in order to do it. It has been estimated that 20 million people died as a result of his reign of terror.

CHINESE COMMUNISM

Russia remained the only communist country in the world until it was joined by China in 1949. Like Russia, China was not ready for revolution in the Marxist sense because it had a largely rural and illiterate population and little industrialization. In the 1920s it was ruled over by a warlord class in a feudal manner. Nationalist and communist groups formed a united front to try to overthrow this class but the alliance fell to pieces after interference from Stalin and Hitler.

After many years of fighting, the People's Liberation Army, under the leadership of Chairman Mao, declared the People's Republic of China in 1949. Again world war had an effect on the civil war that took place. When Japanese forces invaded China in 1937, many people joined with the communists in order to flee from the Japanese.

Chairman Mao wanted to educate the peasants into the ways of communism so he wrote many texts loosely based on those of Marx. These became the basis of Chinese communism and were eventually published in the West as the famous 'little red book'. Chinese communism, like that in Russia, was a distortion of true Marxist thought.

THE COLD WAR

'A spectre is haunting Europe, the spectre of communism' wrote Marx in *The Communist Manifesto*. After World War II the spectre of communism seemed to be haunting the whole world. This was the period of the **Cold War** when it seemed everyone was on the alert for 'reds under the bed'. The Cold War came about as a result of the way that the

world was divided up after World War II.
During the war, the allies – the united Kingdom
and the United States – had been prepared to
support communism in order to prevent the
rise of world fascism. When fascism was defeated, communism was seen as the main threat to
the balance of power. The Soviet Union, as
Russia was now called, and China were seen to
be becoming more powerful . In 1947 President
Truman of the United States made a declaration

KEYWORDS

Cold War: hostile measures between countries that just fall short of actual war.

Domino theory: the American theory of communist takeover and justification for interference in southeast Asian politics.

that the United States was prepared to counter communist expansion
throughout the world. They were worried by the implications of more
communist states arising, not only out of revolution but by the way in
which World War II had been resolved.

* Europe had been divided by peace treaty and many countries there
  came under communist control as part of the Soviet bloc. Berlin
  was divided by the Berlin wall. An 'Iron Curtain' of secrecy was said
  to have come down between Eastern and Western Europe.

* There were fears that communist China would come to dominate
  southeast Asia. It was felt that 'the loss of Indo-China will cause the
  fall of southeast Asia like a set of dominoes'. This was the **domino
  theory** as described by President Eisenhower, at a press conference
  in 1954, and it led to American involvement in Laos, Cambodia,
  North Korea and ultimately to the Vietnam War.

* There were revolutions in South America and Africa against colo-
  nial oppression. Many of the countries involved received aid from
  the communist bloc in their struggle for independence.

The Cold War was largely an imaginary war based on fear and mistrust
that came from deep ideological differences between the East – communism – and the West – capitalism. It came to an end largely due to the
decline of the communist economy in the Soviet Union and the People's
Republic of China.

IS MARXISM RELEVANT TODAY?

Many people see the collapse of communism as proof that Marx is not relevant to the world today. After the Soviet Union collapsed and the Berlin wall came down, communist China became more open to Western influence and its economy is more open to free enterprise. People see the failure of communism as the failure of Marx yet the communism that Marx envisaged has never existed.

What the history of the twentieth century shows us is the power of Marx's ideas to capture the imaginations of the poor and oppressed throughout the world. There is no doubt that his beliefs, or others' interpretations of them, changed the history of the world.

The relevance of Marx to today's society has been debated and discussed by many philosophers, economists, historians and other academics, as well as by fervent Marxists, students and drunks in the pub. Almost everyone has an opinion on Marx even if it is not a particularly informed one. There are three main arguments.

* Marxism is not relevant today at all because it was never relevant. His scientific method was flawed and his economic theory was completely mistaken.

* Marxism is not relevant today because it was a product of its time. The capitalist society that existed at the time Marx was writing does not exist any more. There is no such thing as the proletariat now, so there will be no revolution.

* Marxism is still relevant. The failure of communism in some countries does not indicate that Marx was wrong. In fact he predicted there would be a swing away from his theories and that capitalism would try to fight back before it was finally defeated. The world may have changed, but while the economy is a capitalist one his theories are still relevant.

To deal with these arguments one by one, the first theory is obviously wrong because even if Marx was totally mistaken about everything, many people have acted upon what he said so it must have had some relevance. The second and third theories can both be seen to be correct, to some extent, although it depends on which aspects of his work are being examined:

History

Marx's scientific method of studying history is not really scientific by modern standards. Twentieth-century philosopher Karl Popper believes that there is no real way of proving whether Marx's assertions are true or false as you could in a proper scientific study. Marx did, however, amass and classify a great deal of evidence about past societies and modern social science developed out of his techniques.

Economy

Marx was not a trained economist. Some of his predictions about the economy have proved to be false. For example, he claimed that wages would be pushed down to subsistence level, while, on the contrary, most people are better off in real terms today than they were a hundred years ago. Other assertions have been correct. He predicted that large corporations would come to dominate world markets. At the end of the twentieth century more and more companies merged into large conglomerates including banks, publishers and of course computer software companies. He also predicted that industry would become more and more reliant on technology and that there would be periodic recessions: Both of these predictions have proved to be correct.

Society

Society has changed for the better and, in Western Europe, many inequalities have disappeared. For example, in Britain there are free education and health services for all who need them. The feudal House of Lords has been reformed, heredity is no longer the only criterion for belonging to this law-making body. Although the proletariat as Marx described it does not exist in the same way today as it did during the time in which he was writing, there is still an underclass of the homeless and the unemployed.

Philosophy

Marx is much more relevant to today's world when we look at his philosophy. There are two main philosophical points to be considered. Firstly, human nature is not a fixed thing, but alters with social and economic conditions. This means that society can be changed by altering the economic system. Nobody was aware of this before Marx brought it to our attention. However, the history of the twentieth century has shown that it is not as easy as Marx believed to create the society of equals that he thought could develop. The fact that communist states have been riddled with inequalities does not mean that Marx was entirely wrong, but perhaps he was more optimistic about the flexibility of human nature than most people.

The most important part of his philosophy was the understanding he gave us about the nature of freedom. Under capitalism we appear to be free but, because economic conditions control our work, religion, politics and ideas, we cannot control our lives or society. Is the fact that depression a major cause of absence from work in the United Kingdom in 1999 a symptom of alienation? Of course this is a supposition that is not easily proved, but according to surveys it is true that people are less happy than they were 40 years ago despite an increase in material possessions. The fact that we even acknowledge the possibility of this alienation is because Marx introduced the idea. People are now much more aware of the social and economic influences which shape their lives and this is due, in part, to Marx.

THE FUTURE

The world developed in ways that Marx could not have predicted in just 100 years. Trying to look at the development of Marxism in the next hundred years would be an exercise in science fiction. We cannot predict how technology will change our society. Perhaps work will cease to exist as a result of technological advances; perhaps society will be destroyed by some disaster and we will return to primitive communism.

The revolution Marx predicted has never taken place, but does that mean it will never happen?

Marxists would argue that as long as ten per cent of the population hold 90 per cent of the wealth then there is no equality. There are still numerous Marxist groups in the world which believe that as long as society remains dominated by capitalism then there must be a revolution. As long as the ideas of Marx are still alive in the minds of people throughout the world then this must be a possibility.

* * * *SUMMARY* * * *

• Marx died in 1883 but Engels continued to work on his manuscripts.

• His ideas were spread around the world through the labour movement and working men's groups.

• Marx wrote a vast body of work which has been interpreted in widely different ways.

• Russia became the first communist country in the world after a revolution in1917.

• The Cold War was based on the fear of the spread of communism in the West.

• Communism failed in many countries due to economic problems.

• Many people believe that Marx is out-of-date and not relevant to today.

• Others believe he is relevant because of the inequalities in society and revolution could still occur.

• Marx's main contribution was to show us that human nature is not fixed and that even when people believe they are free, they are being controlled by outside influences of some kind.

TIMELINE 1750–1917

Events In World History		Events In The Life Of Marx	
c. 1750	Start of the Industrial Revolution in Britain		
1775–1783	American War of Independence		
1789–1794	French Revolution		
1800–1815	Napoleonic Wars	c.1818	Karl Marx born
c. 1830	Industrialization of Europe begins		
		1835	Attends University of Bonn
		1836	Attends University of Berlin
1848	Riots in Paris, Vienna and parts of Germany and Italy	1841	Thesis accepted at University of Jena
		1842	Works as a journalist
1851–52	Louis Napoleon declares second French Republic	1843	Marries Jenny von Westphalen and moves to Paris, becomes a communist
1861–1865	American Civil War	1845	Expelled from France and moves to Belgium
1870	Franco–German War	1848	*The Communist Manifesto* published
1871	Paris commune proclaimed. Third French Republic established	1849	Banished from Germany, moves to London.
1905	First Russian Revoltion	1859	*Critique of Political Economy* published
1914	World War begins I	1864	International Working Men's Association founded
1917	Bolshevik Revolution leads to first ever Communist state	1867	*Das Kapital*, Volume 1 published
		1881	Wife, Jenny, dies
		1883	Karl Marx dies.

MARX ON ...

Some extracts from *The Communist Manifesto* 1848

Communism
A spectre is haunting Europe – the spectre of communism.

In this sense, the theory of the Communists may be summed up in the single sentence: abolition of private property.

Communism deprives no man of the power to appropriate the products of society: all that it does is to deprive him of the power to subjugate the labour of others by means of such appropriations.

Class
The history of all hitherto existing society is the history of class struggles.

Freeman and slave, patrician and plebeian, lord and serf, guild-master and journeyman, in a word oppressor and oppressed stood in constant opposition to one another, carried on an uninterrupted, now hidden, now open fight, a fight that each time ended, either in a revolutionary reconstitution of society at large, or in the common ruin of the contending classes.

The modern bourgeois society that has sprouted from the ruins of feudal society has not done away with class antagonisms. It has but established new classes, new conditions of oppression, new forms of struggle in place of the old ones.

Bourgeoisie
The bourgeoisie, wherever it has got the upper hand, has put an end to all feudal, patriarchal, idyllic relation. It has pitilessly torn asunder the motley feudal ties that bound man to his 'natural superiors', and has left no other nexus between man and man than naked self-interest, than callous 'cash payment.'

It has resolved personal worth into exchange value, and in place of the numberless indefeasible chartered freedoms, has set up that single unconscionable freedom – Free Trade. In one word, for exploitation, veiled by religious and political illusions, it has substituted naked shameless, direct, brutal exploitation.

Modern bourgeois society, with its relations of production, of exchange and of property, a society that has conjured up such gigantic means of production and exchange, is like the sorcerer who is no longer able to control the powers of the nether world whom he has called up by his spells.

It has been objected that upon the abolition of private property, all work will cease, and universal laziness will overtake us.

According to this, bourgeois society ought long ago to have gone to the dogs through sheer idleness;

Proletariat
The modern labourer, on the contrary, instead of rising with the process of industry, sinks deeper and deeper below the conditions of existence of his own class. He becomes a pauper, and pauperism develops more rapidly than population and wealth.

But with the development of industry, the proletariat not only increases in number; it becomes concentrated in greater masses, its strength grows and it feels that strength more.

Utopian socialists
...They reject all political, and especially all revolutionary action; they wish to attain their ends by peaceful means, necessarily doomed to failure, and by the force of example, to pave the way for the new social gospel.

Such fantastic pictures of future society, painted at a time when the proletariat is still in a very underdeveloped state and has but a fantastic conception of its own position, correspond with the first instinctive yearnings of that class for a general reconstruction of society.

Industrialization
...Steam and machinery revolutionized industrial production. The place of manufacture was taken by the giant, MODERN INDUSTRY...

Society suddenly finds itself put back into a state of momentary barbarism: it appears as if a famine, a universal war of devastation had cut off the supply of every means of subsistence: industry and commerce seem to be destroyed. And why? Because there is too much civilization, too much means of subsistence, too much industry, too much commerce.

Imperialism

The need of a constantly expanding market for its products chases the bourgeoisie over the entire surface of the globe. It must nestle everywhere, settle everywhere, and establish connections everywhere.

Women

The less the skill and exertion of strength implied in manual labour, in other words, the more modern industry becomes developed, the more is the labour of men superseded by that of women. Differences of age and sex have no longer any distinctive social validity for the working class. All are instruments of labour, more or less expensive to use, according to their age and sex.

The bourgeois sees in his wife a mere instrument of production. He hears that the instruments of production are to be exploited in common, and, naturally can come to no other conclusion than the lot of being common will likewise fall to the woman.

He has not even a suspicion that the real point aimed at is to do away with the status of women as mere instruments of production.

Family

The bourgeoisie has torn away from the family its sentimental veil, and has reduced the family relation to a mere money relation.

Revolution

But not only has the bourgeoisie forged the weapons that bring death to itself: it has also called into existence the men who are to wield those weapons – the modern working class – the proletarians.

The immediate aim of the communists is the same as that of all other proletarian parties: formation of the proletariat into a class, overthrow of bourgeois supremacy, conquest of political power by the proletariat.

GLOSSARY

Alienated Feeling isolated or estranged from society.

Anarchists Believers in the theory that society does not need government.

Antithesis From ancient Greek, meaning negation. Antithesis is the second stage of Hegel's dialectic view of development, when the initial stage, or thesis, is contradicted.

Bolsheviks A branch of the revolutionary movement; originally part of the All Russian Social Democratic Party.

Bourgeoisie The middle classes who developed capitalism and took power from the aristocrats.

Capital Money to which surplus value accrues.

Capitalist An economic system where there is private property and relatively free markets where goods are sold for profit.

Cold War Hostile measures between countries that just fall short of actual war.

Colonialism The second stage of imperialism, where countries take over governing power.

Commodity An object for use that is produced for sale.

Communism A state where private property has been abolished, where people live in equality without classes or social divisions.

Concrete labour Labour that has to be applied to a product to give it use-value.

Democracy A state governed by the wishes of the whole, adult population, where no smaller group has the right to rule. From the ancient Greek *demos* (the people) and *kratos* (strength)

Dialectal materialism Marxist way of studying the relationship between the real world and the world of ideas.

Dialectic The philosophic theory of contradiction and change.

Dictatorship of the proletariat Unavoidable undemocratic state made necessary after communist revolution.

Domino theory American theory of communist takeover and justification for interference in south east Asian politics.

Economic base The way the economy is structured in a society.

Economist A person who studies the science of the production and distribution of wealth.

Economy The system by which wealth is created in society.

Engels, Friedrich Son of a wealthy textile manufacturer. He wrote about the plight of the working class and was a close friend of Marx.

Evolutionary communists Communists who believe a communist state can come into existence through the natural disintegration of the capitalist system, without the need for revolution.

Exchange value The value that commodities have in relation to each other.

False consciousness False beliefs or values created by a culture or society.

Fetishism Desiring, worshipping or giving excessive concern to inanimate objects.

Feudalism A system of land ownership that gave the nobility rights over the land, which they granted to their followers in return for services.

French Revolution 1789–1794. Revolution by the people against the French aristocracy. After a bloody uprising, the nobility were overthrown and replaced by a bourgeois democracy.

Hegel German philosopher (1770–1831. His writings on the progress of civilization influenced Marx and are explained in detail in Chapter 2.

Idealist philosopher One who believes that there is a divine force of some kind which is responsible for the development of the ideas and beliefs of mankind.

Ideology World view; the perception people have of the world around them.

Imperialism Economic and political domination of one society by another.

Industrial Revolution Term used by historians to describe the development of industry, and the factory system that began in Britain around 1750.

Labour Work done to add value to raw materials.

Labour power The strength and skills of the worker.

Lenin Russian Communist leader. Inaugurated the dictatorship of the proletariat.

Little red book Popular name for *The Thoughts of Chairman Mao*. Millions of copies, with a distinctive, red cover, were distributed around the world.

Manifesto Official statement of political intent.

Mao Tse-tung 1893–1976. Founder member of the Chinese Communist party, he became head of state, or chairman, in 1949.

Materialist philosopher One who believes all ideas and beliefs are a result of life in the material world, and not the result of intervention by a divine or supernatural force.

Means of production Raw materials, factories, land, that allow production to take place.

Mercantile capitalism This is the first stage of Imperialism. It began in the sixteenth century when explorers discovered new continents and plundered them. Large companies became the governing power in countries where they settled.

Nationalized Brought under state ownership.

Necessary labour the time the worker spends actually earning the amount paid in wages.

Philanthropy Practical benevolence.

Philosopher A person who uses reason and argument to seek truth and knowledge.

Primitive communism The type of classless society that existed in the distant past when people were hunter-gatherers.

Proletariat The property-less working class in a capitalist system.

Radical A person who wants fundamental change in a political system, usually through altering the basis of society.

Revolution The overthrow of one ruling class by another, resulting in major changes to the structure of society.

Revolutionary communists Communists who believe a communist state can only be created by a revolution.

Socialism In Marxist theory the stage between revolution and true communism.

Sociology The study of society and social problems.

Soviets Regionally elected local councils in communist Russia.

Stalin Russian peasant who became dictator.

Surplus labour the time spent producing surplus value for the capitalists.

Surplus products Products over and above those that satisfy the basic needs of the producers.

Synthesis From ancient Greek, meaning union or amalgamation. The final, third stage of Hegel's dialectic, where the thesis and antithesis are combined.

Terrorism The use of violence to make people accept radical social and political change.

Theory of surplus value Marxist theory that explains how capitalists are able to profit from their workers' labour power.

Thesis From ancient Greek, meaning affirmation. The first stage of Hegel's dialectic, where the original theory, or viewpoint, is proposed

Third world Poor, less industrialized and underdeveloped countries, often former colonies.

Tsar Russian emperor, or leader, of the semi-feudal society that existed before the Communist Revolution of 1917.

Use-value The intrinsic value that a commodity has for its 'usefulness'.

Utopian socialists Believers in a mythical, perfect state.

Vanguard of the proletariat Leaders of the communist movement who aim to educate the proletariat.

Young Hegelians A group of radical thinkers who debated the ideas of Hegel and Feuerbach. Marx was a prominent member in his student days.

FURTHER READING

Works by Karl Marx

Penguin Classics have nine volumes of his works in paperback editions. These include all the major and more important works. The most important works for the beginner to read are *The Communist Manifesto and Das Kapital (Capital)* Volume 1.

Lawrence and Wishart began publishing the *Collected Works* of Marx and Engels in 1975. Eventually there will be 50 volumes, divided into 4 sections-Early Philosophical Works, General works, Economic Works, and Letters. The major and more important works have already been published.

A selection of Marx's writings are available in

The Marx Engels Reader Robert C. Tucker (ed.), WW Norton, 1978.
Karl Marx: A Reader Jon Elster (ed.), Cambridge University Press,1986
Karl Marx: Selected Writings David McLellan (ed.), Oxford University Press, 1977

Works on Marx

* *An Introduction to Karl Marx* Jon Elster, Cambridge University Press 1986, reprinted 1996. An analytical approach to the thought of Marx, written for use by undergraduates and condensed from the larger work *Making Sense of Marx.*

* *Making Sense of Marx* Jon Elster, Cambridge University Press, 1985. A large systematic study.

* *Karl Marx – His Life and Thought* David McLellan, Macmillan,1973. A comprehensive guide.

* *Marx* Peter Singer. Past Masters Series, Oxford University Press, 1980, re-issued 1996. A useful philosophic introduction.

* *Marx* Terry Eagleton. The Great Philosophers Series, Phoenix, 1997. A short work examining Marx and freedom.

* ***Karl Marx*** Francis Wheen, Fourth Estate, 1999. A very readable account of Marx as a person.

* ***Karl Marx: His Life and Environment*** Isaiah Berlin, Fontana, 1995. Originally published in 1939 this is a well known, readable account of Marx.

* ***Alienation: Marx's Conception of Man in a Capitalist Society*** Bertell Ollman, Cambridge University Press, 1977. A readable account of the theory of alienation.

* ***Communism – An Illustrated History from 1848 to the Present Day*** Geoffrey Stern (ed.), Amazon, 1991, A summary of the way in which the ideas of Marx were spread around the world in the various forms of communism. It contains many fascinating maps and illustrations.

THE WRITINGS OF KARL MARX

Marx wrote numerous articles, essays and books throughout his life. These are the major works that contain his most important thoughts. Although many are not an easy read for the beginner, and not all of them are available from ordinary bookshops, anyone who wants to study Marx in more depth should read as many of his original works as possible.

* **1844** *On the Jewish Question.* An essay that is rather anti-Semitic but it sheds some light on Marx's view of the rights of man.

* **1844** *Contribution to the Critique of Hegel's Philosophy of Right.* Introduction. This was intended to be a full critique on Hegel's *Philosophy of Right* but the introduction was the only part to be completed. It is important because it is here that Marx first discusses the importance of the emancipation of the proletariat.

* **1844** *Economic and Philosophical Manuscripts of 1844* – also known as the *Paris Manuscripts.* These were not published until after Marx's death. The main theme of the Manuscripts is the alienation that people suffer in a capitalist society.

* **1844** *The Holy Family or a Critique of Critical Critique.* This was written with Engels as a criticism of the ideas of the young Hegelians. The title is a sarcastic reference to the Bauer family. It was first published in Germany and not translated into English until after the deaths of Marx and Engels.

* **1845** *Theses on Feuerbach.* These are short statements that Marx wrote to show how his materialist philosophy differed from that of Feuerbach. They were published by Engels in 1888.The eleventh thesis on Feuerbach is engraved on Marx's gravestone.

* **1845–46** *The German Ideology.* This was not published until after his death and it was written in collaboration with Engels. It is important because it states the theory of the materialist view of history and further discusses alienation in a capitalist world.

* **1848** *The Communist Manifesto.* Written with Engels, for the Communist League, this is one of Marx's more important and well-known works. The first English translation was made in 1850. It was written as a direct appeal to the workers and so has the feel of propaganda. It describes the capitalist system and the creation of the classes of bourgeoisie and proletariat. It examines the idea of class conflict and calls the workers to revolution. It also gives some idea of how communism could be put into practice.

* **1849** *Wage-Labour and Capital.* This was produced from lectures given by Marx before German working men's clubs in Belgium in 1847. These were later published in *Neue Rheinische Zeitung* as a series that was never finished. Engels updated and revised the work before publishing his translation after Marx died. It explains Marx's economic theories including the growth of capitalism, how wages and profits are determined, and how this affects the worker.

* **1852** *The Eighteenth Bruimare of Louis Bonarparte.* This was originally published in Die Revolution a German language paper published in New York. The 'Eighteenth Bruimare' refers to the date in the French revolutionary calendar on which Napoleon Bonarparte made himself dictator. In 1852 his nephew Louis Bonarparte proclaimed himself as Emperor Napoleon the Third. In this article Marx discusses French politics and history from 1848 until 1851, the date of the coup that brought Louis into power. The article is important because it explains his theories of the capitalist state.

* **1857–58** *The Grundrisse.* These were notes made in preparation for a *Contribution to the Critique of Political Economy and Das Kapital*, and were not intended for publication. They were first published in Moscow in 1931–41 and made available in translation in 1953. They are interesting to study because they show how Marx developed his ideas on economic philosophy and history.

* **1859** *A Critique of Political Economy.* A short piece on economics that is important mainly for the preface, which summarises the theory of historical materialism.

* **1861–1863** *Theories of Surplus Value.* These were contained in notebooks not published until 1906–1908. They are mainly notes for Das Kapital dealing with the historical perspective of economic theory.

* **1865** *Value, Price and Profit.* An address given to the First International Working Men's Association published after Marx's death. It explains most of Marx's economic theory in more simple terms than Das Kapital, including the theory of surplus value.

* **1867** *Das Kapital – Volume 1.* This is Marx's most important work, a long and detailed study of economics and its relation to history and society. It also gives evidence of the ways in which capitalists exploit workers.

* **1875** *Critique of the Gotha Programme.* This was a commentary made on the document that was written during the Gotha conference, when two German Socialist parties became united. Marx felt that the Gotha programme did not adhere to the precepts of scientific socialism. He wrote the Critique in reply, and circulated it amongst German socialist leaders, but it did not have much effect on the unification that took place. It was published after his death and is one of the few places where he discusses the way a future communist society might be organized.

* **1885** *Das Kapital – Volume 2.* This was published by Engels and based on notes that Marx left before he died. It gives more detail on economic theory but is rather dry and boring. Unless you are an academic with a great interest in Marx's economics it is probably not worth reading.

* **1894** *Das Kapital – Volume 3.* This is another work published by Engels from notes made by Marx. It is slightly more interesting than volume 2, but again it is of more use to academic scholars of economic history than to the beginner.